If there's one thing I've learned through my travels
It's that, even after seeing the world,
It is okay to think the most beautiful place is the one in which you started.

Some days I feel not myself
I'm drowning
Hoping my instincts kick in
And I am able to start swimming back to who I was

But for now
I am
Lost
At
Sea

<u>Bipolar lover</u>
I wish I could use a thermometer
To monitor our conversation
So I could know whether you're going to be
Hot or cold

<u>Mythical Creature</u>
You are my unicorn
Something too good to be true...

Or is it because who I think you are
Doesn't actually exist...

I ask myself again and again why I fall back to what broke me
Why I find myself still loving you

But it is because I love myself
Scars and all
And who I am includes the pieces you broke

I want a love where the honeymoon stage
Is not a stage

What is the point of staying once the magic is gone?

I want my eyes to serve as more than just my own
I want the places I've been
The feelings I've felt
To have the same impact on those who can't live like me

It is the reason I put word to this page
And my eye to the lens

The reason I
Write
Photograph
Create

I am living in the now.

-    Don't tell me to put my phone down

Life does not stop for anyone
It does not stop when your heart is aching

And it does not stop when you want more time

<u>The key</u>
You have to find the one that loves the same as you
Or else you'll always be
Too clingy
Too Psycho
Too Needy

That feeling in the pit of your stomach
That's your heart sinking
Because your choice of lover does not know what you need to hear

My heart would break for you over and over again

But it deserves better than someone who would allow that

I love him so much that I get lost in it
And to me
That is the scariest part

To think I could want someone so badly
That I'd be willing to lose myself

These compilations of my thoughts...
Kinda scary isn't it?

You could be reading this and think I'm crazy

but,

I
Dont
Care

He is my dream

But, to him
I
Am
Nothing

Do my words make sense to you?

No?

I guess we don't speak the same language

Make up your mind
I am tired of asking flowers
If you love me
Or not

The older I get the more these damn cliches start making sense

You drown me in your indecision
Until I am left
Feeling unsure of myself too

I am writing a book
                    I am left with nothing
        Just this pen
        This page
        This hurt

Then I remind myself
    This could be
    Everything

& YOU do not define MY worth

Without travel
My life feels like
A conveyor belt
Going on
And on
And on

Same thing everyday
With purpose,
But no meaning

How ironic the term "love sick" is
Because sick is how I feel
You left
And now I am sick

She looks at planes in the sky
Longing to be a part of its journey

Why is it I feel pathetic about the fact
You are my dream

Maybe it is because I am not yours

-Dream Bigger

Do not be afraid to say how you feel
Your feelings
Your opinion
Can never be wrong
They are yours

I want a love so incredible I hate sleep
Because sleep means
Moments missed

I envy those who are able to be fulfilled staying in one place
Settling down

My heart always longs to be
Somewhere else

I'm not here to inspire you

I'm here to make you fucking feel something

I thought I loved your flaws
But looking back
I forced myself to accept them

I was not in love with you
Just the idea
Of you

I miss that summertime breeze
Swaying through the trees
I miss simple days
With you

<u>Mama</u>
I miss the sweet sugar of watermelon on my lips,
&
The sounds of stories
Coming off yours

A thought can be here and gone in an
Instant
But unfortunately for me
You
Are never
That thought

Why don't we brag about ourselves more?

I want to go places
and do things

And I want those things to mean something
To me
To others

I want to look back on my life
And know
I lived
Every bit of it

Life is the longest thing you will ever do
But it is still too short to do anything that makes you unhappy

I knew within days of knowing you
That your love
Would be the end
Of me

You are not a waste of space
You are not a waste of time
How you feel can never be wrong

Say it
Repeat it
Believe it

Social media takes away the mystery

I want my writings to reveal them instead

You can't make someone love you
But
You can make a dog love you

-The Real American Dream

Too often people take for granted the
Passion
They are able to feel

If you have found something
Or *someone*
You are passionate about
Grab onto it
& whatever you do
Do not
Let
It
Go

Not everyone finds it

I am never going to ask you to
Stay
And you are never going to
Stay

So what the hell are we doing?

Sitting at my desk
Reminiscing on photos

I decided

It's time to go back to Europe

Why do I think swearing is so fucking romantic?

Truth is
I have no fucking idea where my path will take me

It could leave me
Poor
Alone
Homeless

But
I'll always have the memories

& to me
That is worth
It all

Snowflakes touch
& melt together

Much like
You & I

You are so
Bad
For me

But you feel
So
Fucking
Good

People always compare love to a drug

I never understood that
Till I understood
You

-Drug Addict

I need to listen to slow music after
You
To slow
Down
My racing heart

I just want to feel
A l i v e

I don't want to think
About tomorrow

All I know is
Right now
I am happy

I want to soak that in

I start living
Around you

There's only so much you can do
To convince someone
Of your
Love

Why is it that
You
Don't trust
ME

You're the one who
Fucked
Up

April first
That's one of your days

As if we had a kid together
Some time is mine
Some time is yours

But this day
This day will always be
Yours

Like the 24th of september

And even though we're miles apart
In more ways than one
I know
Year after
Year
On these days
My mind will flood to you
And what I gave to only you

There's something romantic about a bottle of Jack

I am worth
So
Much
More

You
Do not deserve
Me

Yet...
I give myself
To you
Anyways

I know a lot of people with addictions
Booze
Pills
Love
Attention

My whole life
I thought I was different
Until I met
You

Suddenly
I do everything I know is bad for me
Because
It all leads
Me
To
You

Maybe I did it wrong
Maybe I should have walked
Away
But
When I see that smile
Feel that touch

I'm taken to a different place
Somewhere foreign
Like your accent
& I
Am
Happy

You can make someone want to
Fuck you
But you can not make someone
Love you

You fucked me
And then you fucked me

I'm not trying to be mean
But
You can all
Fuck
Off

These lyrics say
the thoughts
I cannot say
But still,
You will not listen to the song

I'm just the girl who can't
Move on
Who can't
Forget

I am
Stuck

I want to hold you
But
I don't want to hold you
Back
But
I want you to hold me back

Now I understand why writers get blindly drunk before they begin

They need to intoxicate themselves
To the point they will relive some of their toughest memories
And then,
turn them into
Art

I keep trying to force myself to like peppers

They smell good
They look good

But
I just really don't like peppers

I do the same with people
I like just the idea
But try
Time
And time again

I want someone to love me like
Picasso loved his paintbrush

His paint brush made him who he is
With it he created art
Without it he'd be nothing

I accepted a long time ago
That I was not going to be able to be with the man I love.
The one my heart beats for

So
I moved on
I found loves to fill my heart
With joy
Life
Adventure

Instead of searching for a replacement I knew I'd never find
I just looked for people to make me feel
Alive

I want someone
I can count on
Someone
I can talk to
Every
Day
Someone
Who feels the way they say they do
And has actions to support it

And you shouldn't have to change

I miss
You
So much

My heart hurts

We've all heard the cliches about how we as humans create
Homes
Out of people
Rather than places.
I've seemed to make
Homes
Out of
Things

I order mint chocolate chip ice cream and all of a sudden
It's summertime
I'm sitting on a hill named after fruit
With
My best friend

Maybe
We moved
Too fast
Because we wanted to
Feel
So much

Never be worried about being psycho
Stand
The fuck
Up
For yourself

I'm not saying i am better than
Her
I am saying we both deserve better than
You

Not to say I'm fully grown
I'm only 20
But
I'm just now realizing how much easier life was
Back then

How much easier it was
To be with who you love
To hang out with your true friends
Even to get a good night's sleep

All of that seems impossible now

Friends come and go
The man you love coincides with the man you hate
And all of this
Keeps you up at night

I always felt the need to stick around
I was scared of being forgotten

I need to be needed
I need people to need me

You were the right hand man
In destroying one of the
Best
Things to ever happen to me
Because you realized
You
Fucked
Up

You were the guy who taught me how to
Love &
Trust
Not because you gave me those things
But because you were the perfect example
Of their antonyms

My heart
A lit match
My dreams
Gasoline

You've left me feeling
Obsolete

But
Whose fault is that really?

If you ever get lost
Know
I know who you are
And I love you

<u>San Diego</u>
For the first time
In a long time
I didn't wish I was up there
On the plane
Taking off on a journey

I was happy
Right where I was
Windows down
Music playing

People are always telling me to live in
The moment
To stop looking through
My lens

But I'm taking something that lasts
Seconds
And turning it into something to last for
An eternity

My art is my air
Without it
I suffocate
Without it
There is no moment to live in

I don't want to live for
Somedays

I don't care if this makes you feel
Good
I just want to make you
Feel

Why am I with someone who I constantly feel the need to say
Please don't cheat on me to
I
am really cheating
Myself

Do people
like you
exist?
Are people
Like you
Real?

Go ahead and tell
Me
That
My
Art isn't good enough
That
My
Poems do not meet
Your
Standards.

That's the funny thing about art.
What
You
Think
Does not change the
Artist's
Meaning

I don't want to write too much about
Love
I don't want you to think it consumes
Me

But really what else is there?
Money
Jobs
Things
They all fade and they will not fill your aching heart

It is all about
People
And your connection to
Them

Do you ever have those moments
Where you feel like
No one
Fucking deserves you?

I believe that everything happens for a reason
And that there is fate

But what if I don't want to be with the person I'm destined for?

Is that possible?

You read all these quotes about how
Your someone
Is out there...

Is that a sweet nothing
Everyone
Tells
Everyone
So that we have some sense of hope?

-The Human Condition

How can I hate my past
When that past
Has led me to my present

Stop running away from
Moments
Take in every bit

You must
Feel
To be alive

I take a photo of myself
Because I look good

I delete the photo of myself
Because no one's good
Enough
to see

You say you
Love me

But I think you are saying it for you
To cover up the guilt
You feel
For the wrong
You have done

I think about ending it
To make you feel my pain

But the worst part is
That would hurt
Me
More than it would hurt
You

You wouldn't even care
Because
You
Never
Did

My mouth won't say how I feel
So my actions will have to do it instead

I can't figure you out
What do you want from
Me

Sometimes
I'll say I'm going to bed
And lie awake for hours
Alone

Because being alone is easier than talking to you

Going home always reminds me of two things:
I'm glad it is there
&
I'm glad I am not

I want a love that sticks to me
Like peanut butter in my mouth

Can home be home without my people?

I don't care what I go through
Or how many times my heart breaks
Onc thing will always stand true:
I believe in love

It's all golden
The hair
The hour
The moment

But nothing gold can stay

The saddest thing is
I wonder if you'll even miss me

Some girls can put up with it
But I'm not some girl

In the morning he makes a pot of coffee
Which neither of us drink
We just like the smell

-Mexico

You deserve to never question whether or not you are loved ever
Ever again

I don't think anyone can find
The one
Until they are okay with the idea of being
Alone
Forever

Now I don't know if I believe in fate
I begged for it to make our paths cross

Maybe it doesn't know we are meant to be together

But I do

You are driving
Me
And everyone who has to hear me talk about
You
Crazy

I should have known
You ~~were~~ are an addict
Love is your one of your vices
You take a hit and once it wears off you move on

Leaving me like the needle

You deserve to feel like a fucking
Queen
Or
King

If you are with someone that makes you feel otherwise
Walk away while your crown still fits

It is not your fault
You are not overthinking
It is not your anxiety
He
Is
Trash

If a man has you picking apart other woman and pointing out their flaws
Leave him

After all the years of traveling
Of searching the globe for herself
She came back to the place she first started
With the man she first loved
And knew someday was finally here

-Happily Ever After

We sat and we stared with the wind in our hair
Knowing this memory would be burned in our minds forever
Like the stars in the sky

-Santa Monica

Sol searching while I'm
Soul searching

My heart is torn in two
Not the way it is when you end up with someone
Who doesn't know how to love
But a different kind

I leave, I travel, I wander
All the while time passes by
Life is short and family is all we have

I know they want me to see the world
But all I want is to see them

I never knew how easy it was to make your dreams come true
If you want to be something it is as easy as being it

People believe otherwise
Because they are searching for some form of validation
That they are living their dreams
Like money
Love
Praise

But the reality of it is, if you want to
Be something
Do something
It
Just
Is

<u>How can you be so cruel</u>

You left me alone
Crying into my pillow
So I wouldn't have to tell my friends that
They
Were
Right

My mind is left wondering why
Is there someone else
Why wasn't I good enough
But I'll never know
I wasn't even good enough to know

<u>Actions speak louder than words</u>
I kept begging for you to say something
But your silence should have said enough

Maybe if I put these words on paper
I'll no longer feel the knife dragging through my heart

And after it all
I still don't think they were right
You may have fucked me over
But at least I still got fucked

How could you just disappear
To not have the decency to give someone you loved an explanation
Nothing
It
Just
Stopped

The world is a really fucking lonely place
If you're not careful
You will find yourself filling voids with people who dont deserve it
Just to assure yourself you won't be alone
But because they're the wrong person you will end up
Lonelier

I tell myself all the time that I don't know what I want
Which a lot of the times is true
I never know what I want for dinner
I couldn't pick a movie to save my life
And I'm all over the damn place when it comes to a career

But there are a few things I know I want
I want to be close with my family forever
I want to nourish my relationships with my best friends
Because they are some of the most amazing people I've ever met
And lastly
I want real love
A love that understands me
That trusts me
That believes in me
That sees all the things I love about myself and then some

Hardwired to self destruct

The Bathroom Mirror

I look at her and smile
Crooked teeth
Acne scars
Cellulite
She is everything I want to be
She is me

I am no flame in the wind
I am a fucking forest fire
It's going to take more than
You
To put me out

<u>JLL</u>
I have always believed everything happens for a reason
Like life, death, and the changes of season
There are a million reasons God gave me you
To always have support no matter what I go through

<u>Love Destroys/Love Heals</u>
My mother used to play music all the time
Cleaning, driving, relaxing, it was constant
like thunder after lightning

For years after my father's mistake
My mother couldn't listen to music anymore
Not in the car
Not in the house
Not on TV

It wasn't until she married Jim
That she could ease her ears back to the music
That's how powerful love is
It can hurt so bad that it takes away your constants
Your knowns
& turn them into something
Unbearable
Or
It can be so good that it restores you back to the better version of yourself
Back to who you used to be
But better

<u>Compassion</u>
I found myself censoring my writing to spare people's feelings
Even though they didn't spare mine

Once I fell in love with myself
It seemed as if the world fell in love with me too

I think that everyone is just lonely
We all want someone to talk to
To justify our existence
To need us
But no one needs us more than ourselves

<u>True Beauty</u>
Live your life so you have more moments
Where you feel beautiful without looking in a mirror
Like when you're leaning out the window
& the wind is blowing your hair back during the golden hour
Or when you're sitting in a cafe alone reading a novel
Make more of those moments

I spread myself too thin
Like when there's only a spoonful of jam for two pieces of toast
But still I did not feel like I was doing enough

The truth is, I was doing too much
Because it was the wrong thing

<u>I love you, Dad</u>
I used to get angry at my father
For asking me everyday when I am coming home
It made me feel guilty
When all I was doing was trying to grow and live my dreams

But then I realized
How lucky I am to have someone who thinks about me everyday
When you've been raised with good parents
You forget that it is a privilege to have people who think about you everyday
Remember that
Not everyone is as lucky

<u>Mom</u>
You gave me love
You gave me trust
You gave me home
You gave me friendship
You gave me life
You gave me everything

<u>Bro Bear</u>
You took whatever form i needed you to
Brother
Parent
Friend
Thank you

<u>Sis</u>
The lessons you have taught me are infinite
I look up to you in every way
You make me want to be a better person
The world needs more people like you

List of Yes

Before I go to sleep every night I ask myself if I am happy
If the answer is no I ask myself
Why
If the answer is yes I ask myself
Why
I have a running list of both
Guess which one keeps growing?

<u>Him.</u>
Someone thought you were worth dying for

<u>My weakness</u>
Why is honesty so hard
Why do I feel like I can't be honest in fear of hurting someone's ego
The truth is burning in my throat

<u>Tuesday After Work</u>
You asked me to watch your things while you went outside
I thought to myself why you would ask such a thing since it was only
You & I
In the cafe

The reality was there was a room full of people
But my eyes could only see you

<u>Our Love</u>
Like rain in San Diego
Rare
Short
& sweet

It's tearing up my insides
To not put my thoughts to this page
In my attempts to create more positive poems
I've forgotten what this is all about

I can't sensor my feelings

<u>You Can Run, But You Can't Hide</u>
I'm doing what any person who struggles to maintain happiness would do
Overlooking the truth for temporary joy

<u>This Must Be Euphoria</u>
Smiling all the way home
Tracing my fingers across the parts of me you've kissed

I am so proud of who I am
Where I came from
All the parts that make me whole
So much so
That the opinions of others mean as much to me
As a penny to a millionaire

Can it be enough to just want to end up with someone so badly?

It took me a long time to realize
That walking away would hurt much less
Than staying with the wrong person

I thought I was going to love you forever
I thought there was nothing you could have done
To make me fall out of love with you
But then you broke my heart
And now the spaces between the pieces cannot be filled by you

I could have loved you so good
If only you had let me

<u>Moving on</u>
You've got to realize it's not going to fade over time
Unless you actively decide to
Move on
Every single day

<u>Home</u>
Going to B&N with my mom and sister
Eating for an entire army at my grandparents
Movie marathons with my brother
Grocery shopping & holding my dads hand on the car ride home
Going to the lake with my best friend

I'm at a time in my life where it feels like
A movie
Right before you know something life changing is about to happen
And I can't wait

I get butterflies
Thinking about a time
When you can kiss me goodnight
Every night

Every day with you
Feels like the beginning
Of the rest of my life

I don't want to rush into anything
But I feel so alive

I need to be needed
But you just want to be wanted

Sometimes I find myself thinking
I'm not working hard enough
Or doing the most responsible thing
Because my life feels like a vacation
Then I think, why can't life be that sweet?
There is no reason it can't be reality

Look at the regrets of the dying
Then go live

<u>There's more to life than love</u>
Once upon a time there was a girl
Who loved a boy so much
That she still managed to be her own person
And live her life for herself

All while
Loving
Him

We've been off and on for so long now
I keep my faith in the idea that if we are meant to be
It will happen
And if we are not
We will both meet people who make that clear

<u>When I lost you</u>
I lost a part of myself
I lost my art

<u>When I lost you pt. II</u>
But my art is not gone
It is just hiding
Behind my broken heart
And it will be restored

I want
Someone who feels the way you say you do

<u>Ich Liebe Dich</u>
He never would even have to say the words I love you
and I would know he did
Just by the way he holds me at night

You're never too old
Or young
To fall in love

<u>Sailor</u>
You chose to love what was convenient
Because you're too scared of
Commitment and
being alone

You took things I didn't know you could take

I'm scared I am going to spend the rest of my life
Looking for someone or something
To make me feel as alive as you did

SCD

I wish you could see the brilliance I see
Perfectly imperfect
I look up more to you
Even though you think you look up to me

It's not the end
But the beginning
Of letting go
Of thoughts
Heartbreaks
Disappointments
But more importantly,
the opinions of others

-This is Not A Poetry Book

Made in the USA
Columbia, SC
07 December 2018